I0767754

How To Stop Being Reactive

The Ultimate Guide on How To Stop Being Emotionally Reactive

Patrick Anna

Copyright © by **Patrick Anna**

All rights reserved. No part of this publication may be reproduced, distributed, or transmitted in any form or by any means, including photocopying, recording, or other electronic or mechanical methods, without the prior written permission of the publisher, except in the case of brief quotations embodied in critical reviews and certain other noncommercial uses permitted by copyright law.

Table of Contents

Chapter 1

Understanding Reactivity

Emotions are an inherent element of being human, and they play a significant role in our lives. They help us connect with people, express ourselves, and make sense of our surroundings. However, our emotions can become overwhelming at times, causing us to respond in ways that are neither helpful nor productive.

This is when regulating emotional reactivity comes into play. The intensity and speed at which we experience and communicate our emotions are referred to as our emotional reactivity. When we are overly reactive, our emotions might take over, resulting in impulsive behavior and feelings of anguish. However, with experience and awareness, we may learn to control our emotional reactivity and respond to it in a more balanced and productive manner.

A complicated psychological idea known as "human reactivity" governs how individuals react to different stimuli and situations. Some people appear to be readily provoked by relatively minor incidents, while others appear to remain cool and composed in similar situations. It is crucial to note that reaction is a normal element of human behavior and does not always imply a mental health problem.

The Function of Neurobiology in Reactivity

The brain plays an important part in human reactions. The amygdala, a small almond-shaped region in the brain, processes emotions, particularly fear and anxiety. When people face situations or stimuli that they perceive as frightening, the amygdala activates the body's fight-or-flight response, causing increased reactivity. Some people may have a more sensitive amygdala, which makes them more likely to react strongly to even tiny triggers.

Neuroimaging studies have indicated that the amygdala's sensitivity to emotional stimuli varies between individuals, implying that neurobiological factors influence reactivity. Furthermore, studies on anxiety disorders show a link between amygdala activation and greater sensitivity to perceived threats.

Psychological Factors and Reactivity

Personality qualities, past experiences, and cognitive processes all have an impact on human reactions. Individuals with specific personality qualities, such as strong neuroticism, may be more vulnerable to emotional reactions. Furthermore, past traumatic events might cause emotional triggers and sensitivities, resulting in increased reactivity in similar situations. Cognitive distortions, such as catastrophizing or all-or-nothing thinking, can magnify perceived threats, resulting in more intense reactions to insignificant situations.

Neuroticism and emotional reactivity are positively correlated, according to studies. Furthermore, research on trauma survivors has shown that previous experiences can cause hyperarousal and emotional responses, even in non-threatening contexts.

Sociocultural Effects on Reactivity

Sociocultural influences can also influence human reactions. Cultural standards, social expectations, and the environment in which people are reared can all influence how they express and cope with emotions. For example, certain cultures may encourage emotional outpouring, resulting in greater response, whilst others may promote emotional reserve.

Cross-cultural research has revealed considerable disparities in emotional display and responsiveness among cultures. These distinctions indicate that societal influences shape emotional reactions.

Human reactivity is a complex phenomenon influenced by a variety of psychological, neurological, and social variables. While some people appear to be more reactive than others, such reactions should not be labeled as abnormal or symptomatic of mental health difficulties. Reactivity is a natural and adaptive response that differs between people based on their backgrounds and experiences.

Understanding human responses can help people develop empathy and communicate more effectively in a variety of social situations. Individuals can better moderate their response by emphasizing the importance of emotional awareness and good coping methods. By encouraging open discourse and respect for individual diversity, we can build a more compassionate and understanding society.

Chapter 2

Promoting Self-Awareness

Individuals who lack self-awareness do not have a thorough grasp of their own personalities, feelings, motivations, objectives, desires, or behaviors. These individuals frequently experience difficulty in terms of personal growth and establishing healthy connections with others. They may struggle to recognize their own values, moderate their emotional reactions, receive criticism, listen to others, use empathy to guide their behaviors and communicate vulnerability.

For example, someone who lacks self-awareness may feel defensive when given constructive comments, engage in more negative behaviors, and under or overreact to emotionally difficult situations. Frequently, persons who lack self-awareness are contrasted with those who have carefully acquired this attribute. Self-aware people may explore their inner selves, define their personal values, recognize their emotional impulses, and grasp how their actions affect others.

As a result, self-awareness can help people make better judgments, form stronger, more trusting relationships, exercise greater personal control, communicate more effectively, and successfully collaborate with others. With these advantages in mind, strengthening this quality can help professionals achieve greater success in their careers while also cultivating happiness in their lives.

Increasing Your Self-awareness

While growing self-awareness can take a significant amount of time and effort, there are several ways you can use to achieve this goal. Here are eight tips to help you enhance your self-awareness.

Think before you react

Understanding your emotions and being able to control your impulses are important aspects of being self-aware. As a result, strive to be attentive to how you react to external stimuli and consider your response alternatives before acting. This can help you become more deliberate in your interactions with others and guarantee that you respond appropriately, especially in difficult situations.

Be open to hearing and incorporating feedback

You may be able to improve your self-awareness by requesting input from people you trust. Try to be as open as possible while receiving comments on your behavior or performance, whether it is constructive or slightly unfavorable. The insights you gain during this process can help you identify areas for improvement, gain a better knowledge of how others see you, and practice successfully controlling your emotions.

Reflect on who you are

Self-awareness frequently necessitates in-depth reflection on one's identity, both personally and professionally. It can be useful to spend some time analyzing your inner self, define your basic values, and decide what is most important to you. It may also be beneficial to question your preconceived assumptions and investigate why you believe them.

Consider how your actions affect others

External self-awareness is the understanding of how your activities affect others and how they may see you. As a result, when engaging with friends, family, and coworkers, try to be careful of your actions and think how they could interpret them. From here, you may improve your ability to recognize suitable methods to engage and form healthier, more productive interpersonal interactions.

Identify triggers for negative feelings

If you struggle to control your negative emotions and frequently become locked in a loop of reaction, it may be beneficial to investigate what causes these sentiments. Understanding your triggers might help you gain insight into yourself and improve your emotional intelligence. For example, some people who lack self-awareness become triggered when they lose control of a situation, and learning why this is the case might help them avoid such urges.

Keep a journal to record your thoughts

Connecting with your inner self helps increase your self-awareness. Consider keeping a diary to record your ideas, reflect on your experiences, process your emotions, and gain a better understanding of the events in your life. This method can help you develop a greater sense of self-assurance. Furthermore, you may be able to utilize your writing practice to create objectives for yourself and measure your progress as you achieve them.

Develop your listening skills

Those with a strong sense of self-awareness are generally mindful of how much space they take up in a group environment. Furthermore, they may be genuinely interested in hearing what others are saying in order to get insight from their talks. With this in mind, it may be beneficial for you to focus on establishing tactics for improving your listening skills so that you can interact with people more successfully.

Immerse yourself in new experiences

When attempting to increase your self-awareness, it can be beneficial to step outside of your comfort zone and embrace new, challenging experiences that force you to understand more about yourself and how you fit into the universe. Try to follow this approach and engage in activities that will help you transform your mentality. For example, you could explore visiting a foreign nation or pursuing a new interest.

Chapter 3

Emotional Intelligence

Emotional intelligence is the ability to engage with others' emotions while also understanding, managing, and expressing one's own. It requires empathy, or the ability to experience what another person is feeling. However, it also includes other talents such as dispute resolution and rapport building, as well as the capacity to control one's own emotions.

Developing emotional intelligence (EQ) focuses on relationship skillfulness, as opposed to intellectual intelligence (IQ), which is concerned with cognitive ability. Those who understand emotional intelligence can receive information, process it, and respond with understanding and compassion. They are outstanding listeners, proactive rather than reactive, and are frequently effective in crisis situations, all of which help them succeed.

Emotional intelligence is a powerful predictor of success in business and life. Managers who understood emotional intelligence displayed skills such as effective leadership, self-confidence, and the capacity to win and influence others. Interestingly, the winning managers obtained good ratings from their peers and supervisors but not from their subordinates. Despite the appearance of emotional intelligence in the organization of peers, the managers' EQ was not visible to subordinates.

As much as we are taught to appreciate intellectual pursuits, it is our ability to feel emotions, build relationships, and display strong character that leads to opportunities in life. Because connections are at the heart of business and life, understanding how to develop emotional intelligence is more important than increasing your intellectual capacity. It is that crucial.

How to Increase Emotional Intelligence

Learning how to develop emotional intelligence requires a certain perspective. You must change your mindset so that you can control your emotions, thoughts, and actions.

Develop a deep belief in yourself

When you sincerely think that you can overcome any obstacle, you will develop unstoppable confidence, which is essential for learning how to build emotional intelligence. To gain confidence in any scenario, recall a time when you effectively dealt with a comparable feeling. If you have done it before, you can do it again, thinking about previous triumphs allows you to confidently cross unknown terrain.

Rehearse how you want to deal with challenging emotions in the future to prepare for confronting them. Leverage your prior successes to enhance your emotional intelligence. Being prepared strengthens your confidence in your ability to handle future obstacles.

Learn emotional management techniques

Psychology Today discusses the importance of emotional intelligence in navigating life and relationships. To truly understand how to enhance emotional intelligence, take control of your own feelings. Improving emotional intelligence entails keeping calm under stress rather than becoming reactive. To remain calm during a crisis, recall the comprehensive nature of your peak state. To stay calm, focus on your body at the current time.

Identify what you're actually feeling

Recognizing one's own feelings is the first step toward becoming emotionally savvy. Dig deep and ask yourself how you actually feel. Mindfulness is a tried-and-true method for gaining perspective on your feelings, allowing you to regulate negative emotions while harnessing positive ones. As you become more aware of your emotions, you may pay greater attention to how you communicate with yourself and others.

By paying close attention to the words that you use, you can develop empathy for other people, which in turn strengthens the relationships that you already have and opens the door to the formation of new ones. The more emotionally acute you are, the more resilient you will become to challenges as you continue to develop. You can grow and recover from misfortune rather than allowing it to completely consume you.

Receptive to the emotions of others

Emotional intelligence training can alter the way you interact with other people. Your ability to build healthy connections with other people is enhanced when you are in tune with your feelings because it makes you more aware of the feelings that other people are experiencing. You can understand the concerns of other people, identify emotional cues, and have comfortable conversations with other people. When you can satisfy your own emotional needs, you become a spouse, friend, coworker, or family member who is more emotionally open to others.

It is impossible to genuinely comprehend the feelings of other people without engaging in attentive listening. Most people think of listening as waiting to answer. While the other person speaks, they are formulating their argument or relating the conversation to themselves. That does not constitute true listening. Deep listening requires acknowledging and seeking to comprehend the other person's point of view, rather than simply answering with your own.

Assert yourself

Being assertive does not equal being aggressive or domineering. The most productive and healthiest communication style is assertive communication. It does not involve getting in people's faces; that is an aggressive communication style. Assertive communication means expressing your thoughts or emotions in a forceful, confident manner while respecting the viewpoints of others.

Asserting yourself is part of learning how to improve emotional intelligence since it requires you to convey your opinions, desires, and requirements directly while still respecting others. As you develop more aware of your emotional geography, you'll be able to assert yourself in ways that enrich and deepen your relationships.

Get excited and take action
A true decision is defined by the fact that you made a new action. To properly learn how to increase emotional intelligence, you must put your talents into practice. Set a new goal or milestone, then track your progress. Step out of your comfort zone. Engage in more meaningful discussions with the people in your life. Be more present.

Acknowledge and cherish your feelings
Improving emotional intelligence does not require suppressing your feelings. Your feelings are never incorrect. They are there to support you, so be upfront about your feelings. When you learn to accept your own feelings, you will be able to validate the emotions of others, which is a key element of practicing empathy.

Approaching your feelings with curiosity allows you to pause your existing emotional trajectory and solve whatever is upsetting you. When you are open to your emotions, you may better grasp your own and others' thoughts and reasoning.

Maintaining awareness of your mind-body connection allows you to overcome stress and stay connected to others. Allow yourself to take a break if, after coping with your stress, you still need to express harsh emotions such as anger, fear, or grief. As your emotional skillfulness increases, you will be able to better govern yourself and relate to others.

Consider finding a mentor, joining a mastermind group, or obtaining coaching to help you enhance your emotional intelligence. Place yourself in circumstances where emotional intelligence is vital. When you put your emotional mastery to work by being attentive to others, you will be rewarded in your personal and professional relationships.

Chapter 4

The Power of Pause

A pause is an intentional slowing down that creates space between input and response. We can relax by pausing because it activates the parasympathetic nervous system. When our nervous systems are calm, we have more ability to reject habitual reactions and instead adopt a more satisfying, effective, and situationally appropriate response.

My first epiphany about the changing influence of pausing occurred when I felt frustrated with my list-bound behavior. I was always moving like a freight train, trying to accomplish my list of self-imposed and other-imposed obligations. As if by not stopping, I'd ultimately move through the list and be able to relax. This was a foolish undertaking. So I decided to run an experiment and take 7 minutes between each thing on my list. I couldn't believe what transpired in seven minutes.

I got the opportunity to feel what I was drawn to achieve next on the list, and even better, a lot of items on the list became less urgent, or I realized they were things I could easily outsource to someone else. My list shrank, and I became more aligned and pleased with my obligations. Here is the documentation for using your internal pause button.

Recognize the trigger
Take note of when sensations begin to build up inside you. Maybe it's a rising body temperature, a pulse in your head, a knot in your stomach, or a tightness in your chest.

Recognize these triggers as cues to push your internal pause button. During a dispute, note how your ego rises to defend its stance. A simple awareness of the ego is sufficient to subjugate it and send it crawling back into its hiding nook.

Press pause
Mentally say, "pause," as if grabbing for the remote.

Take deep breaths
Getting a small burst of enhanced oxygen to your brain allows you to organize your thoughts and stay in the current moment.

Observe
Simply wait and listen when dealing with people. No rule mandates you to say something immediately. Notice the thoughts that cross your mind and simply observe them without attachment. To avoid impulse eating or spending, remember back to a goal you set for yourself in this type of situation or a slogan you created. Move onward to the finest conceivable outcome. What outcome do you want this to have? Allow yourself to simply watch your thoughts.

Press play
You are now ready to act. Mindfully. I know what you're thinking: That sounds wonderful in theory, but it will take too long in the heat of the moment

Yes, it may feel like that at first. If you're predisposed to respond immediately, convince yourself that it's good to wait.

It helps a lot to give oneself a few more seconds before responding. Pressing the pause button allows you to rewind, make a good decision, and then press play again to advance in a better approach.

It empowers you to make sensible decisions and take command of your life. By talking less and listening more, you may create deeper relationships and learn a lot more. Just because you think it does not mean you have to voice it.

Pausing as Self-Care

Learning to halt is a personal gift of self-care. Taking little pauses during the day helps to ease tension. More spaciousness and less concern and urgency create much-needed space for enjoyment and amazement. We can work harder while feeling happier and more relaxed.

When we move too quickly or don't take time to pause, we can easily misuse authority because our habitual reactions trump our abilities to pick a more considered answer. When we transition from one topic or technique to another in class, I frequently encourage my pupils to pause and take three deep breaths. The pause offered by taking three breaths offers some purification and the ability to make space inside for the following thing. I am so enthusiastic about this that I believe it is unethical for someone to be too busy to take three breaths.

When we move too quickly or don't take time to pause, we can easily misuse authority because our habitual reactions trump our abilities to pick a more considered answer. When I face an issue, I generally have an immediate solution in mind. When I take three breaths before answering, I enable the resolution to emerge in a more creative and inclusive approach.

Pause In Relationships

Pausing is also a useful relationship method, although it is not as simple as it may appear. It takes a startling level of self-awareness to recognize a habitual tendency you commonly deploy in relationships, and then to allow yourself some space before reacting and choosing an alternative answer. When I can halt and wait a little longer than usual, it allows for something new or deeper to emerge.

Effective use of connection pauses is an excellent leadership skill. It was vital not to step in too quickly to handle an issue. You could spend all of your time handling one calamity after another. Instead, create some opportunity for others to share their opinions and let a creative and collaborative solution grow.

Ways To Use Pausing In Daily Life

Using pauses successfully is one of the most fundamental secrets of being power-positive. Here are some specific experiments to try. For one week, try at least one of each experiment. Make a note of the outcomes at the conclusion of the day. Harvest your results.

- ❖ *Pause in your relationship world: Decide to wait longer than typical before conversing.*
- ❖
- ❖ *Pause in your personal world: intentionally choose to leave space between chores.*

Slowing down isn't always simple. If you are too stressed or overwhelmed to find time to relax, consider seeing a therapist who can educate you on how to manage stressors and cope with overwhelm.

Chapter 5

Let Go of Control

People feel safer in uncertain situations when they have a sense of control. This frequently results in attempts to manipulate outcomes, events, other people's conduct, or the environment. The more unexpected the situation, the more people strive to impose control.

In fact, the opposite is true. To acquire the greatest sense of tranquility, peace of mind, and control over one's future, a shift in thinking is essential. The change is toward a worldview that values self-efficacy over regulating external conditions.

Self-efficacy is the belief that we can accomplish what we set out to do, regardless of the conditions. It expresses our belief in our own ability to persevere through difficulties. This transition entails letting go of our urge to control the outcome. The emphasis is instead on our inner worlds of thinking, vision, and emotional management.

The value of letting go of control

When you recognize you can't control external conditions, you can redirect your energies elsewhere. You can concentrate on the only thing you have control over your thinking, attitude, and viewpoint. You acquire self-confidence by letting go of the need to control external factors. This leads to enhanced physical and emotional health, as well as increased strength and mental fitness.

You will increase your work performance as well as feel more joyous and free. Letting go of what you can't control opens the door to new and exciting possibilities.

The Art of Surrendering

Surrendering to the unknown could be frightening. Most people interpret surrender as a sign of vulnerability. This is founded on the concept that we know the correct road and how to get there.

But what happens when something unforeseen or unfixable occurs? These include a pandemic, the illness or loss of a loved one, or a big shift in your employment. In essence, surrendering demands strength and guts. The entire acceptance of "what is" and "faith" that everything is good even without my interference.

Surrender literally means to abandon fighting. Don't argue with yourself. Stop rejecting the universe and the natural order of things. Stop resisting and straining against reality. Surrender does not mean inaction. It is about acting from a point of abandoning energy.

Letting Go in Times of Uncertainty

Change is defined as an external occurrence. These include downsizing or restructuring, illness, death, and changes in social connection or community. Transition refers to the internal work that people perform to assimilate change and realign themselves in the face of change. Success stems from focusing on the inner transition. That is, true achievement requires a focus on inner work.

Personal growth occurs when you struggle through a difficult issue, push yourself beyond your comfort zone, and embrace the great and negative feelings that come with it. Here's how you do it.

Endings

The first step in transition is to let go. When people acknowledge that something has ended and acknowledge their losses, the first stage of transition starts. Losses may be both obvious and hidden.

A new job could, for instance, mean losing a previous identity or a sense of camaraderie with former coworkers.

This is where you decide what to let go of and what to hold onto. You may hold some things loosely, some tightly, and let some go because they are no longer helping you. Many people become stuck here because they do not go through the assessment process and lack the fortitude to let go.

Neutral zone
After letting go, the transition continues. This is the neutral zone, or in-between phase when the old has passed but the new has not yet fully manifested. This is when you learn who you are in the new reality, possibly mourning your old self and figuring out how to "be" in the new beginning.

The neutral zone is not fixed in length. Many people make the mistake of hurrying through the neutral zone because they are uncomfortable with uncertainty or the unknown. This is where the power of letting go takes root and opens up new possibilities. self discover the new self: what you enjoy, what you want to do more of, and what you want to stop doing.

New beginnings
Beginnings involve new knowledge, values, and attitudes. You've realized your new identity. Transitions that are well-managed allow you to step into new responsibilities with a clear sense of purpose.

You will gain a better understanding of the role you play and how to contribute to the new world. Many people go immediately into a new beginning, such as a new job, without thinking about the ending or passing through the neutral zone. This can lead to a decline in satisfaction with the new position. Achieving a smooth transition requires dedicating time to endings and neutral zones.

How to Let Things Go

Letting go is more an art than a science. But there's good news. You may learn skills to help you navigate change and uncertainty. These help you understand what to hold onto and what to let go of.

Focus on what you can control

You have no influence over external events or how others react. You only have control over your thoughts, attitudes, responses, and reactions. You must learn to believe that events beyond your control will unfold as they will and that everything will turn out for the better.

There are several approaches for establishing trust, and not all of them are effective for everyone. Some people find that their religious faith allows them to let go of control. Others place their trust in the universe or fate. Others have learned from experience that most uncontrollable circumstances resolve themselves in a constructive way. They may elect to place their reliance on pure statistical evidence. Do whatever works for you.

Do not rush through the transition

Fully accept endings and acknowledge your losses, especially if they are failures. Consider what to keep lightly, what to hold securely, and what to let go of that is no longer useful to you. Allow yourself to consider options and possibilities instead of a specific outcome. This is where your new beginning could unfold right in front of your eyes.

Be in reality

You may dislike the change around you, but ignoring it will not change it or help you manage the shift. Adopt a mindset that completely accepts the new reality. Don't wonder how you can turn it back. Instead, ask yourself: "How will I respond now that this has happened?

Identify your triggers

Identifying the triggers that motivate you to control external occurrences provides you with information. You can then utilize interventions to disturb your cognitive process and modify your perspective.

Notice any stiffness in your body or an increase in anxiety responses. This is an especially effective strategy for dealing with trauma-related discomfort. It allows you to avoid situations that may cause a stress response. Take steps to relax and soothe your body and mind.

Get in contact with you
A lot of practice gives your mind room to adjust to the change. These assist you in successfully adjusting. Whichever option you select, as long as it suits your needs, is acceptable. A few concepts:

- ❖ *Spend time outside in nature.*
- ❖ *Do a physical activity that you enjoy.*
- ❖ *Practice conscious breathing.*
- ❖ *Meet with friends or loved ones and focus on developing a meaningful relationship.*

Try something new.
Allow yourself to dream of prospective futures, and carefully watch how you feel when you think about these possibilities.

- ❖ *Engage in mindfulness meditation as a way to remain present.*
- ❖ *Use positive affirmation as a source of inspiration and control over negative thoughts.*
- ❖ *Do what offers you delight, and you will lose sight of time.*

It's time to let go of control
It can be tempting to want to control everything in your life. The trouble is that if you don't learn to let go, you'll quickly find yourself overwhelmed by fear, wrath, and unpleasant emotions. You may struggle to keep track of all of your responsibilities and controlling behavior. Remember these five steps for letting go and overcoming a control issue. You will be flooded with happiness and inner calm.

- ❖ *Focus on what you can control.*
- ❖ *Do not rush through the transition.*
- ❖ *Be in reality.*
- ❖ *Identify your triggers.*
- ❖ *Get in contact with you*

Chapter 6

Integrating Non-Reactivity Into Daily Life

Every feeling has a reason to exist, as the hit film Inside Out convincingly demonstrates. It's pointless to suppress our feelings or be annoyed by anything in particular. Joy is wonderful, but anger, sadness, fear, and disgust all play a role and allow us to see into our minds. An unpleasant mood arises to indicate that something needs to be addressed. I'm sad because I'm mourning and I need my pals. I'm concerned since this assignment is difficult and will require additional time to complete. Recognizing emotions and what they represent in our lives is valuable in and of itself for keeping us on the correct track for ourselves.

However, not every emotion is triggered by real-life experiences. We all experience ups and downs. Moods can be transitory. Some arise as a result of our own internal chemistry. Nonetheless, we frequently blame external factors for these erratic mental states. We assign a mental breakdown on our employment, our partner, or some other external experience; someone or something must be to blame. We unintentionally push people who could supply us with comfort away when we need it. If he really cared, he would come sit with me, but I haven't asked and I've been as prickly around him as a cactus. In our perceptions, someone has become a part of the problem, and our actions reinforce our suspicions.

Sometimes our mood is simply our mood. We may seek solace in a reactive behavior, such as withdrawing from or lashing out at others; both can be beneficial when done purposefully, but not so much when done reflexively and without thought. They frequently provide temporary relief without addressing the underlying reason, especially if it isn't fixable to begin with. We can also become fixated on maintaining the status quo, such as getting caught up in the final moments of an ideal vacation while still on the beach.

Sometimes there's nothing else to observe except how we're feeling and, for a while, letting life be. I'm shaken, and there's nothing I can do about it at the time. A mood appears and disappears on its own, no matter how dreadful or great it feels, and the healthiest thing for us to do or think about may be nothing at all.

When we neglect to pay attention to emotion, we warp our perception of the environment, exacerbating displeasure. When we are furious, we are more inclined to see people as angry. Sadness, anxiety, and other emotions influence our perceptions. Our emotions influence how we think, which in turn undermines our emotions. Both ideas and emotions influence how we physically feel, which in turn determines our emotional state. That cycle will continue uninterrupted unless we make an effort to steer it in a better direction.

When we develop awareness, we may observe our feelings more clearly and with less resistance. We notice our thought patterns and intentionally opt to leave things alone for a moment.

Negative feelings, more than positive ones, capture our attention and refuse to let go. They initiate processes that lead us further into mental rabbit holes. Oh crap, here I am again: I'm incapable of caring for myself, or similar thoughts compound already difficult mental situations. What was supposed to be a brief slump turns into a crisis due to a mental cyclone caused by dread, guilt, and self-doubt. That mental storm overwhelms us, and we shun activities, people, and even modes of thinking that would normally make us feel better.

By practicing mindfulness or other techniques that raise awareness, we can more easily and objectively notice our emotions. We notice our thought patterns and intentionally opt to leave things alone for a moment. I'm in a foul mood; it's not my fault nor anyone else's, and it will pass. Regardless of whether we want to ignore or react to emotion, we work on something new. We pursue effective and healthy ways to release overwhelming emotions. For the most part, we may observe, seek consolation when possible, and then plan the next solid step forward on a tough day.

Mindfulness Practice

This meditation focuses on working with habits. In particular, our habitual reactions to challenging situations occur frequently. These could include rage at being stalled in traffic, grief at not obtaining what you desire, or impatience while dealing with companies who keep you on wait for what seems like a lifetime. Whatever it is, whether it is something major or seemingly insignificant, mindfulness techniques can help us deal with our habitual reactivity more effectively.

Meditation for Exploring Your Habitual Reactions
Get into a comfortable position that you are familiar with and that you employ when practicing, and pay attention to your body. If you're sitting, pay attention to your points of contact, such as where your sitting bones rest on your chair or cushion or where your feet or legs make touch with the surface.

Whether your hands are folded into your lap or resting on your thighs, take note of their position in relation to your body. Pay attention to your chest rising, your chin aligned with your navel, and your tongue resting behind your teeth. If you choose to lie down for this activity, it is best to lie on your back.

Pay attention to where your body makes contact with the mat, floor, or bed. Take note of your places of contact as well as the areas of your body that are not in contact. Whatever your position, allow the surface on which you are sleeping or sitting to do the work of supporting you. Pay attention to the front body, the back body, and everything in between.

Now focus your attention on the sensations of breathing that are most readily available, whether at the nostril, chest, or abdomen.

Concentrate your attention on the sensations of the breath as they present themselves to you, focusing on one area in particular.

Pay attention to both the inhale and exhale. Pay attention to the movement of the body as the air flows in and out. Pay attention to the nostrils; you may notice the coolness of the air as it enters and the warmth as it exits. Focus on the breath or the chest, noticing how the body expands with the in-breath and deflates as the breath leaves.

Allow the body to settle. Allow your breath to calm. Breathe in, breathe out, in, and out. Every breath is a new breath. Each breath represents both receiving and releasing.

Your concentration will occasionally shift to thinking, planning, anxiety, or daydreaming. Your role is merely to notice this regular mental inclination and softly return to your breath repeatedly, without judgment or tale. There is no right or wrong here; simply pay attention to your breath, notice when your attention shifts, and bring it back again.

Take note of when the breath is low and when it is brief. Note when it is shallow and when it is deep. Mindfulness is about becoming aware of our entire experience, whether desired or unwanted and in this case, becoming aware of the experience of breathing.

Breathe out and let go of your primary concentration on the breath, allowing it to be there but in the background. Establish focus throughout your entire body when inhaling. Bring an open mind to the experience and sensations in your body as they come and go. Take note of their arrival, persistence, or passing, and investigate them. Bring a positive attitude and curiosity to this exploration of the sensory basis of experience, whatever it is.

Observe how your body feels. A region of your body may feel comfortable, tense, relaxed, uncomfortable, or painful. Whatever it is, when a sensation demands your attention, analyze it and discover its depth and various features. Whether you lean into it or lean away, whether it is good, bad, or neutral, without changing anything in this now, simply pay attention to what arises in your body as it manifests.

Attend to what arises as best you can without judging it, but be aware of any judgment or aversion that arises. Explore the sensation as objectively as possible.

Investigate experiences as they occur. Once you've done exploring one sensation, wait for another to appear and investigate it. Remember that sensations might be internal or external. Perhaps sounds are making themselves heard as they come and go. Get to know your body's sensations right now.

Take note when your attention shifts to thinking, or when you feel compelled to act or change positions. Recognize that this is what is present right now. Re-focus your attention on your body repeatedly. Explore one sensation, let it go, and then focus your attention on another when it enters your awareness.

Now, if you want, imagine a tolerable stressful situation. Perhaps you've recently been frustrated, unhappy, puzzled, or anxious. Perhaps it was an issue in a relationship or at work. Keeping this circumstance in mind, remember that if what comes up becomes too much for you, you can always return your focus to breathing with your body.

If your eyes are closed, then open them. Consider a stressor and observe what happens instantly. It could be a physical sensation, a cognition, or an emotion. Perhaps there is a behavior or inclination to act. Begin to understand your stress reactivity signatures.

If you have any thoughts, try to observe them as carefully as possible. If there are emotions, try to name them, such as "sadness" or "anxiety." Remember that labeling your emotions helps to calm them and make them more controllable. Labeling emotions gives you the power to choose what occurs next.

If you have any bodily sensations, take note of them and pay attention to them. Explore them, even if they are unwelcome. Get to know them. Stay with them as long as they have your attention. Take note of whether they increase, persist, or dissipate. Recognize that this is a stressful situation and that it is fine; it has already occurred. Bring compassion and kindness to this encounter. Accept the situation as is, even if it is unpleasant. Explore your body and sensations for as long as they are present.

Now return your focus to the feelings of breathing, possibly in your stomach. Keep your attention focused on any leftover sensations. Engage in the option to expand into them on the in-breath, softening, expanding, and letting go on the out-breath, letting go, or allowing and letting be, if feasible. Just pay attention to the rising and falling of the breath as it arrives and departs in your abdomen, if this is not essential.

Expand once more around the breath to include all sensations throughout the body. Be present with your body, breathing in the background and emotions in the foreground, from head to toe. Bring a sense of vastness to your experience by remaining open and responsive, with an open front and a powerful rear.

When you're ready, stop doing this and try to live in the next moments with a broader, more expansive awareness.

Now, if you feel inclined, take a piece of paper and a pen and write down any words, thoughts, feelings, bodily sensations, or urges to act that occur to you. Write down what happened in that practice when you introduced the stressor. Name and list your emotions. What body sensations and urges to act or behaviors, if any, crossed your mind? These experience components can manifest themselves in a variety of ways, ranging from thoughts to emotions, body sensations, behaviors, and back to emotions and thoughts, and that's fine. Keep a record of these when they appear.

After you've completed, take time to review what you've written and consider where in your habitual reaction you could intervene with mindfulness. How could you raise awareness of these habitual behaviors when they occur, allow more choice if necessary, or introduce alternate options for how to respond? How might you stop yourself so that you can step back and get perspective?

Pay Mindful Attention to Habitual Reactions
Perhaps make a promise to yourself about how you will practice this in some little way when hardship occurs. Perhaps once a week or once a day, simply pay careful attention to an experience, recall the breath when trouble arises, shift an attitude, or engage in a different behavior. Whatever you do, remember that awareness is always just a moment away, and mindfulness is portable; it can accompany us wherever we go, at any time.

Chapter 7

Maintaining Inner Peace

Both inner tranquility and the external surroundings are essential for well-being. Surroundings influence flourishing. Inner serenity comes from within, whilst the environment shapes us from the outside. Seeking both is vital. We all want to experience more peace, tranquility, and joy in our lives. Inner tranquility appears to supply a unique type of life fuel, whether it's easing stress, feeling grounded, or distributing positive feelings.

However, in the pursuit of spiritual growth and enlightenment, it might be tempting to focus completely on the inner journey, foolishly believing that external forces will have less influence once our mentality evolves. We might convince ourselves of the myth: that "A peaceful mind can survive anything." "I don't need perfect conditions to find happiness!" It may work for extremely enlightened sages, but not for the majority of us.

True, inner serenity gives a solid basis, yet we cannot overlook how much our surroundings influence us. If our surroundings are toxic, they can sap our vitality and weaken the inner reserves we have worked hard to build. Your exterior world reflects your inner world. What happens inside you is reflected outside of you. Let's go deeper into their interconnected dynamic.

The Stable Core
When life becomes hectic and reactive, turning inside brings stability. We realign with our essence by quieting our worried thoughts through continual spiritual practices such as meditation, writing, nature walks, and more. Our tumultuous emotions have settled into peace. We regain perspective and learn how to respond consciously rather than reactively. We are rooted in something greater than the emotional storms caused by momentary conditions.

When we connect with our inner calm, we discover the wisdom that helps us navigate storms or sunshine outside.

Cultivating inner tranquility strengthens spiritual muscles, allowing them to resist being tossed around by external situations. Our centered core is constantly present, guiding us home. We can access it through joy and grief, stability and change. This inner tranquillity allows us to weather outward storms with empowered resilience rather than a hopeless response. We still experience the whole gamut of human emotions, but we see unpleasant ones with compassion before they dominate us.

So, while inner work does help establish an anchored mindset on which to rely regardless of external events, it does not make us immune, as I can attest from personal experience.

Toxic environments drain the inner reserves
Here's the catch: no matter how well-insulated you are, surrounding negativity creeps in over time, requiring great energy to repel its destruction of our inner light. Regardless of how internally evolved you are, if you are consistently surrounded by poison, it will eventually get to you.

Chronically toxic settings can exhaust even the most grounded and evolved beings. Inner tranquility strengthens us, but it does not make us immune to ongoing psychological assaults. Consider having to repeatedly reaffirm that the sky is blue while everyone else believes it is crimson. Despite your unwavering lucidity, it takes constant mental work to refute their consensus day and night. You dig deep to keep your reality stable, yet it is exhausting and draining.

This is what poisonous conditions eventually do. They push us to draw from our spiritual stores more frequently than we can replenish them, and to what end? Our inner light begins to wane, not from a lack of inner practices, but from constant exterior erosion. As the saying goes, even a single drop may carve rock over time.

It is simple to obtain enough vitamins and minerals from within; it is the pollutants from outside that are problematic. The same goes for spiritual health. Enough inner connection offers nutrition, but outer toxicity depletes them.

Healthy soil enables roots to flourish
Fortunately, the opposite is also true: healthy outside surroundings allow inner tranquility to flourish! A supportive environment not only relieves stress but also actively gives nourishment for our entire being to thrive.

Think of a thriving garden. External conditions that assist plants to thrive include rich, healthy soil, adequate air and sunlight, and well-regulated temperature and moisture levels. If they are planted in poor, depleted soil with little food from their surroundings, they will not thrive properly.

Our spirit acts in a similar way. Inner practices sow the seeds of serenity and tranquility, but they grow exponentially faster when the external conditions allow for full flowering. Similarly, when we are in a peaceful setting, we can thrive. When others with whom we connect show optimism, it is mirrored inwardly. Thus, while inner peace provides sanctuary from challenging environments, healthy environments actively promote more plentiful inner peace, not merely for survival, but also for resurrection.

Peace comes from within. Do not seek it without. This insight provides a foundation for beginning to seek. However, one of the reasons monks and hermits retire to beautiful and tranquil places is that stillness is extremely beneficial to their journeys.

An empowering context involves more than just keeping our heads above water. In order for seeds with human potential to blossom into a blooming, flourishing garden, it actively provides the rich, nourishing soil, sun, and rain.

Cells thrive in a healthy, life-affirming environment but deteriorate in a toxic, life-depriving environment. When we change the internal or external environment from harmful to healthy, cells and people can go from barely surviving to lavishly flourishing.

The Middle Way Between Extremes

Does this imply that we should focus primarily on shaping our environment because external factors have such a significant impact on internal states? Of course, not! As previously discussed, inner calm is important as a steady baseline from which to begin orienting, and the best way falls between both extremes, i.e. actively developing both inner and outside serenity. Developing inner anchoring through conscious outward impact.

This integrative method is dubbed the Middle Way for good reason! Maintaining a balance between internal and external influences promotes long-term well-being. Most of us cannot simply sit in happy inner worlds while disregarding the outside context in which we exist, nor can we attempt to control all outward variables while our own mind spins impatiently or is caught up in unending chatter and turbulence.

The spiritual path is not intended to skip normal human existence, but rather to enable us to gracefully enjoy, luxuriate in, and dance with it. To thrive, we require a stable inner refuge as well as a helpful outer community.

The best course of action is to actively work toward creating and fostering harmony in the environment around you while continuing to cultivate inner serenity via spiritual connection. Raise the collective vibe by making a kind contribution. Support conscious communication, empowered cultures, and evolving systems.

The contextual 'growing conditions' we occupy determine whether we live a coping or thriving existence. Transform toxic settings into enabling ecosystems, and coping methods become thriving superpowers.

Inner labor and outside change alone are insufficient for fostering serenity. We must strike a balance between our influence and our controllable circumstances. As a result, continue to plant and nurture seeds of peace within yourself while also working to create more tranquil situations around you. Strive to preserve inner anchoring while realigning outwardly.

Conclusion

Life is a complex fabric of emotions, and as humans, we encounter a kaleidoscope of emotions that bring depth and color to our existence. However, emotional responses can occasionally mislead us, resulting in impulsive reactions and undesirable behaviors. Compassion, self-awareness, and mindful activities are essential for developing emotional resilience and becoming less emotionally reactive.

Identify triggers

To become less emotionally reactive, understand the triggers that elicit strong emotional responses. These triggers differ from person to person and may be linked to previous experiences, phobias, or stressors. Identifying these triggers allows us to better understand ourselves and anticipate prospective obstacles, giving us the ability to respond more effectively.

Develop healthy coping mechanisms

One of the most important aspects of emotional resilience is the development of good coping skills for dealing with strong emotions. Engage in things that provide you joy and relief, such as exercise, creative outlets, nature walks, or mindfulness meditation. Developing a toolkit of positive coping techniques allows us to manage emotional upheaval in productive ways.

Practice empathy

Empathy is a transforming component in developing emotional resilience. By attempting to understand and validate the emotions of others, we form relationships that foster empathy within ourselves. Empathy for others helps us recognize the universality of emotions, which aids in the development of self-compassion and understanding of our own emotional responses.

Communicate effectively

Improving our emotional intelligence is crucial for becoming less emotionally reactive. Learn how to effectively convey your emotions and wants by using "I" phrases in a non-confrontational manner. Encouraging open and honest communication promotes healthier interactions and can result in better outcomes in difficult situations.

Embrace emotional awareness

The first step in developing emotional resilience is to become aware of your emotions. This includes taking the time to identify and recognize our feelings without judgment or suppression. Instead of pushing them away, allow yourself to sit with your emotions and investigate their causes. By acknowledging our feelings as authentic and worthwhile, we establish a secure environment in which to better understand ourselves.

Practice mindfulness

Mindfulness is a wonderful technique that can help us stay in the present moment and avoid automatic emotional reactions. Mindfulness methods, such as meditation, deep breathing exercises, or grounding techniques, can help us maintain our composure during emotional storms. Observing our emotions without attachment allows us to obtain clarity and make conscious decisions about how to respond.

Pause before responding

When emotions are high, the urge to act swiftly might be overwhelming. However, in order to cultivate emotional resilience, we must pause before responding. This period of reflection allows us to step back from the emotional intensity and reconnect with our inner wisdom. By taking this breath before reacting, we allow ourselves to reply deliberately rather than impulsively.

Celebrate progress

As we work toward emotional resilience, it is critical to recognize every step forward, no matter how tiny. Embracing change requires time and work, and celebrating our accomplishments provides inspiration for future improvement. Celebrating accomplishment fosters a sense of self-worth and emphasizes the positive influence of our efforts.

Seek support and guidance

Navigating emotional reactivity can be difficult, but getting help from trusted friends, family, or professionals can be quite beneficial. Talking about our feelings with others can help us gain new perspectives, validate our experiences, and get advice on coping tactics. A supportive network can provide a secure place to share emotions while receiving empathy and understanding.

Learn from Setbacks

Everyone is susceptible to emotional responses, and setbacks are a normal part of the learning process. Rather than berating ourselves for these situations, consider them opportunities for growth and self-improvement. Accept setbacks with empathy and curiosity, knowing that they are stepping stones to emotional resilience.

Being less emotionally reactive is a humane process that involves patience, self-awareness, and thoughtful habits. Accept emotional awareness, practice mindfulness, and create healthy coping techniques to help you navigate your emotions with ease. Develop empathy for yourself and others, and increase your emotional intelligence via effective communication. Seek help when needed, and remember that setbacks are stepping stones to success.

Celebrate each step forward with compassion, understanding that emotional resilience is a worthwhile journey. When we practice emotional awareness and compassionate reactions, we open the door to increased emotional resilience, empowerment, and inner serenity.

www.ingramcontent.com/pod-product-compliance
Lightning Source LLC
Chambersburg PA
CBHW070750260726
48660CB00007B/3056